Brice Marden

Serpentine Gallery, London
17 November 2000 – 7 January 2001

Director's Foreword

Julia Peyton-Jones

We are honoured to present at the Serpentine Gallery this exhibition of paintings and related works on paper created by Brice Marden over the past decade, which include the recently completed *Attendant* series seen here in its entirety for the first time. This exhibition is the first in-depth presentation of Marden's paintings in the UK since his exhibition at the Whitechapel Art Gallery in 1981.

We are privileged that Brice Marden accepted our invitation to present his work at the Serpentine, and we cannot thank him enough for making this exhibition possible. He has been remarkably generous, participating fully in every aspect of the project, and by doing so has ensured that this presentation reflects both his and our vision for the exhibition. This commitment, which has extended to the loan of works from his collection, has carried this exhibition forward and we have benefited greatly from working with him. Furthermore, Brice Marden generously offered to donate a limited edition print on the occasion of this exhibition, and we are indebted to him for providing the Gallery with the opportunity to benefit from the sale of this work.

Brice Marden's US representative, Matthew Marks, has offered invaluable support to the exhibition from the moment of its inception. We are most grateful to him for his unfailing involvement and his advice on numerous occasions, both of which have greatly facilitated the organisation of this ambitious project. We are equally indebted to Doris Ammann, Thomas Ammann Fine Art, the artist's European representative, for her kind assistance in a variety of ways, and to both dealers for their contribution to the opening celebrations marking the exhibition.

Brice Marden's new works will be a revelation not only to those unfamiliar with his work, but also to those who have followed his career from its early days. We are therefore especially grateful to the lenders to the exhibition, who have generously entrusted these important works of art to our care. In many cases they have made an exception in lending to the Serpentine Gallery and it is a tribute to the artist that they have agreed to do so.

Harry Cooper, Associate Curator of Modern Art at the Fogg Art Museum, Harvard University, has contributed an analysis of the *Attendants* to this publication, placing these paintings in the context of Marden's oeuvre as a whole, and of this exhibition in particular. We would like to thank him for his thoughtful and elegant reading, which adds greatly to our appreciation of

Brice Marden, and also Herman Lelie for the care he has taken with his handsome design for this publication.

We are especially grateful for the support that this exhibition has received from many sources, and would firstly like to extend a very special acknowledgement as well as thanks to Edwin C. Cohen and The Blessing Way Foundation, who agreed to significantly support the exhibition at an early stage of its organisation. As a long-time admirer of Brice Marden, his generous donation has enabled us to realise fully our plans for the exhibition. Gap Inc. have given important and much appreciated financial assistance which has made a significant difference.

We would also like to thank AXA Nordstern for their generous contribution, as well as for lending their professional expertise. Frances and John Bowes have expressed their admiration for the artist through their donation, which is greatly appreciated. The Serpentine Gallery has been in receipt of a gracious anonymous gift, which has also contributed significantly to the realisation of this exhibition, for which we are most appreciative. In addition, we would like to thank our media sponsor, the *Daily Telegraph*, for ensuring that news of the exhibition reaches as wide an audience as possible.

The following individuals assisted at critical moments in the development of this exhibition and we have welcomed their help, advice and encouragement: Peter Bass, Michael Bloomberg, Stefania Bonelli, Maria Brassel, Simon Callery, Gregory Eades, Ingrid von Essen, Dan Hamilton, Tina Hejtmanek, Hans-Michael Herzog, Claudia Kishler, Uwe Kraus, Peter W. Marx, Claire Pardy, Jessie Rosenberg, Sarah Sands, Laura Satersmoen, David Scully, Zoe Starling and Robin Wiley.

Not least my thanks go to Lisa Corrin, Chief Curator, who shaped the exhibition in close collaboration with the artist; Leigh Markopoulos, Exhibition Organiser; Michael Gaughan, Gallery Manager, and to the entire team, who have all contributed towards the successful presentation of this exhibition.

Lenders to the Exhibition

Francesco and Alba Clemente
Daros Collection, Switzerland
Froehlich Collection, Stuttgart
Hirshhorn Museum and Sculpture Garden, Smithsonian Institution
Collection of Ninah and Michael Lynne
Brice Marden
Helen Marden
Melia Marden
PaineWebber Group, Inc., New York
Patricia Phelps de Cisneros
Private collection, Baltimore MD
Private collection, San Francisco
Dr Paul and Dorie Sternberg
Paul F. Walter
Kunstmuseum Winterthur

and those collectors who wish to remain anonymous

Looking at Brice Marden

Lisa G. Corrin

It has been almost twenty years since the influential exhibition of Brice Marden's paintings, drawings and prints from 1975–80 was presented at the Whitechapel Art Gallery in London. Although an important exhibition of Marden's prints was presented at the Tate in 1992, no exhibition of his paintings created during the intervening period has taken place in the UK. The present, tightly focused exhibition, organised by the Serpentine Gallery, attempts to chart the cadences in Marden's artistic production of the past decade. It begins with Marden bringing his extraordinary *Cold Mountain* series to closure and concludes with the *Attendants*, Marden's most recently completed body of work. This exhibition is intended to enunciate and also to build upon the significant contributions made to our understanding of the artist's work by *Brice Marden: Work of the 1990s: Paintings, Drawings, and Prints*, the comprehensive travelling exhibition organised by the Dallas Museum of Art, Texas, last year.

The period following the Whitechapel exhibition has been a fertile one for Marden. From 1988 to 1991, he completed *Cold Mountain*, the line-based gestural abstractions that marked a distinct departure from his earlier minimal panels.[1] These lyrical works with their subtle spatial complexity were inspired by Asian calligraphy and landscape painting. Produced using a paint brush with a long handle, the strong sense of movement, the immediacy of his gestures, and his integration of the unexpected drips of paint, recall the work of another American abstract painter, Jackson Pollock, who Marden acknowledges as a critical influence on his work of the 1990s. Indeed, it seemed to the Serpentine Gallery to be timely to consider this heir to Pollock's legacy just one year after the major presentation of Pollock's work at the Tate. Marden's own work has been of critical importance to the current generation of young painters working in Britain today including Mark Francis, Callum Innes and Simon Callery, to cite just three.

Marden has always seen his work as participating in a dialogue with that of other artists across the history of art. Painting part of the year on the Aegean island of Hydra, over the past decade his interest in Greek sculpture and architecture, as well as its history, landscape and mythology, has deepened. One can see these references in the monumental painting *The Muses* (1991–93), for example, not only in its title, but also in the structure, which moves from calligraphy to choreography, as though a frieze of Zeus's nine children is dancing across its surface. Marden has recounted the influence of Robert Graves's *The Greek Myths* on this work, 'I remember reading Graves and he talked about these bands of reveling, orgiastic maenads that conducted these wild, primal dances in the forest. Later they became the Muses. I was interested in their early stages, and that's where the first Muses painting came from.'[2] Similarly, there is an impulse towards figuration in drawings of this period, such as *Venus #2 (Negril)* (1992–93) with its suggestion of the limestone Venus of Willendorf (30,000–25,000 BC), which becomes increasingly legible in his six most recent paintings, the *Attendants* (1996–99).[3] In these works, lines open up to infer sculptural form. The surfaces are simplified while the forms delineated by interlocking lines are increasingly complex.

Self-imposed principles or structures govern each body of Marden's work. The column-like 'characters' in his later *Cold Mountain* series, such as *Cold Mountain 2* (1989 – 91), 'read' up and down like the ancient Chinese calligraphy found in poetry, but also spread web-like across the surface as in the paintings of Pollock. In *Kalo Keri* (1990), ("summer" in Greek), and *Presentation* (1990 – 92), the lines are rendered in an increasingly complex way and Marden adds colour to the near monotone palette of black, blues and greys of the *Cold Mountain* works, further defining each circuit of interweaving lines. In the *Attendants* the palette is reduced to a narrower range of colours set against a grey ground. The eye follows an almost elusive network of linear forms within a shallow space weaving round and inward and out again. A complex jigsaw-effect is created by a series of linear entanglements in which the forms overlap while retaining their own integrity. Although drawing has been at the centre of Marden's work throughout the 1990s, it is no longer a threshold through which he must pass to paint. It *is* painting.

Standing before any of Marden's paintings makes one acutely aware of the discipline and concentration he employs – many take at least several years before he feels they are resolved. Time is suspended within his working practice and also in the 'narrative' of the work. Despite his use of descriptive titles, which sometimes provide a clue to the source of a work, (*The Muses* with its allusion to Greek mythology, and *Skull with Thought*, pertaining 'to the shape of the head with an idea inside it') or even the hint of figuration, as in the drawing *Venus #2 (Negril)*, it is the legibility of Marden's working process that provides a sense of unfolding narrative.[4] Moreover, the candour with which that process has always been exposed – in his early encaustic paintings with their surfaces built up layer by layer, and their resulting elusive colours, or in the undisguised drips and *pentimenti* of the works throughout the 1990s – sets him apart from many of his contemporaries working in cool, minimal abstraction. The taciturn disposition visible on the surface of Marden's paintings divulges, as in a diary, the artist's restless decision-making process – to make a painting is to make decisions, to both lose oneself and to be acutely self-conscious.

Marden's paintings, at once raw and refined, reveal the precarious balancing act performed by painters in which a tightrope is stretched tautly between their materials – paint, canvas, stretchers – and their process. Looking at the edges of his earliest encaustic panels as well as the sides of the unframed works, one sees the thickened evidence of this dialogue in the density of the coloured planes and their soft texture, as though colour is suspended on the framework of the surface. In later works, the 'narrative' comes alive in the nicks, smudges, erasures, rubs, paint dribbles and *pentimenti* incorporated into the work. But Marden's unusually demanding and intentionally anxious working practice is not merely a process, it is the subject of the work. In this he has a kindred spirit in Cézanne.

The bones of Cézanne's compositions expose themselves, as though his brushwork has flayed the body of the landscape. What they expose is, of course, not a mountain in Provence, but paint. Landscape was a vehicle for 'realising', a term used by Cézanne, who took what he saw and, rather than struggling for a mythical verisimilitude, absorbed the landscape into the substance of paint, in order to transform the natural world into the artificial space of the canvas.[5] To 'realise' was to question and explore the flat surface, the consistency of his material, the formal language of art – composition, colour, line, planarity, scale. Gone are the atmospheric and linear perspectives of earlier art. In Cézanne they are replaced by construction, a building of form from the inside out through a limited palette that unites surface marks, hatching, patterns and contours. His work challenges the relationship between perception and reality and queries the very nature of looking as it affirms the capacity of painting to communicate in a way that is absolutely singular.[6]

Marden's work, like that of Cézanne, begins with observed and felt experiences, and he invites us, the viewers, to enter the same passage of realisation, of faith lost and found. By retaining and making both transparent and productive, the surface by-products of his process, he gives us the most privileged kind of information with which to engage his work. We experience his to-ing and fro-ing first hand, the constant vacillation that leads to the finished work.

While Marden's current work, with its strong reliance upon line, may appear radically different from the monochrome encaustic works of the 1960s and 1970s for which he first received critical attention, the artist's aesthetic position has remained constant. He has maintained his conviction that painting can continually renew itself. His work arises from a willingness to cast doubt over his own practice during the painting process. His unequalled capacity to struggle within self-imposed constraints in order to exceed them has resulted in works of art that may be counted amongst the most aesthetically challenging and inscrutable in the history of abstraction. I recently asked the painter Simon Callery how to look at these perplexing works. 'Dilate the eyes,' he advised, 'and let the body be sensitive to the experience. Don't scrutinise. Let the eye go only so far. Let the information slowly bleed. The point of making this kind of painting is that it's counteracting amnesia. The making is the work.'[7] Marden's willing descent into uncertainty to make his work, 'I like to make things that I don't understand from a point of view of not understanding,' – is cathartic. The degree of his uncertainty is also the measure of his faith in painting to re-fresh itself, and, one might add, his faith in the viewer to look, that is, to follow the trail he has left along the way.[8]

Notes

1
The seminal work on this subject is Brenda Richardson's *Brice Marden: Cold Mountain*, Houston: Houston Fine Art Press, 1992.

2
As quoted in Charles Wylie, *Brice Marden Work of the 1990s: Paintings, Drawings and Prints*, Dallas: Dallas Museum of Art, 1999, p. 25.

3
The comparison to the Venus of Willendorf is Wylie's. Ibid., p.35.

4
Suggested by Wylie. Ibid, p. 42.

5
Yve-Alain Bois has discussed eloquently Cézanne's notion of *réalisation* in the context of Marden's attitude towards his own working process. See 'Marden's Doubt', in *Brice Marden Paintings: 1985–1993*, Kunsthalle Bern and Wiener Secession, 1993, p. 67.

6
The private view card for Brice Marden's 1970 exhibition at the Bykert Gallery was a photograph of the artist atop a marble plinth engraved with *Cézanne*'s name emphasising his belief in the ongoing dialogue of artists working in the medium of painting, a continuum in which he sees himself participating.

7
I am indebted to Simon Callery for this insight into Marden's work.

8
Quoted in Bois see, 'Marden's Doubt', p.67. This analysis is indebted to Bois's now classic reading of Marden's working process.

Brice Marden
Tang Dancer
1995–96
Oil on linen
180.3 × 83.3 cm
Private collection

Marden Attendant

Harry Cooper

Any exhibition of new paintings by Brice Marden is now an 'event', and rightly so, for he is both a slow painter and a good one. In this exhibition the highlight is six new paintings, the *Attendants* of 1996–99. These works (together with four *Sepia Drawings* of 1991–2000 and three *Untitled Red and Green Drawing*s of 1998) constitute the latest news from Marden. They will be the focus of this essay though, of course, responding to new work means responding once again to older work. This interpretive circuit is both inevitable and, given Marden's concern with continuities in his oeuvre, appropriate.

Marden has toyed all decade with the emergence of recognisable objects from within his meandering lines of paint, often using titles that trigger a figurative response (*Sisters*, 1991–93; *Tang Dancer*, 1995–96; *Bear*, 1996–97), but at the same time changing course in a painting if a figure seems to be emerging too clearly. 'It was reading too much like a head so I had to take it out,' Marden said recently of *Study for the Muses (Eaglesmere Version)* (1991–94/1997–99).[1] 'I hedge too much on this issue of subject matter,' he admits slyly, not indicating which side he feels he should come down on.[2] He thinks about 'natural objects turning into, and not quite turning into, abstractions.'[3] (Note that he says *and*, not *but*.) 'You can read them as figures.'[4] (If you want to.)

But this time, it would seem, the case is clear: six new paintings, all titled *Attendant* (one of them with the subtitle *Monk*), all of them vertical, with identical dimensions. 'I always figure that my vertical paintings are figure paintings, and the horizontal ones are landscapes, and the square ones are abstract.'[5] The shapes made here by Marden's looping patterns are clearer than ever, and the different colours of line easier to distinguish. Indeed, before we know it, we start seeing human figures, although admittedly somewhat amoeba-like. So these are the Attendants of the titles. Or are they?

Regarding titles Marden has confessed, 'Some painters refuse to title paintings – they're just numbered, or "Untitled" – because they believe that a title leads you into it in a certain way, which is no good. I've always been very romantic about titles.'[6] In other words, he is not afraid to give us a handle, confident that the complexity of the painting will resist any nominal fixation. But hold on: let's not forget that a title itself may be complex, polysemous. And here I want to insist, perhaps perversely, that we understand 'attendant' not primarily as a noun, 'one who waits on another', but as an adjective, 'an accompanying thing or circumstance, a consequence or concomitant', as in 'attendant circumstances'; and equally (switching to French) as a present participle, 'waiting', as in *en attendant Godot*.

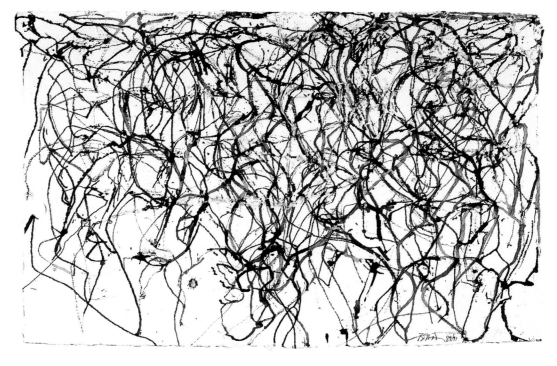

Brice Marden
St. Barts 11
1989/91
Ink and gouache on
handmade paper
27.3 × 40.6 cm
Private collection
Courtesy Matthew Marks
Gallery, New York

These two senses of 'attendant' have in common a certain dependence: a consequence is dependent on its cause, and one who waits is dependent upon an arrival. In both cases there is, as the Latin root of 'attendant' graphically suggests, a stretching towards, *ad-tendere*; and, with the shared sense of dependence, there is also a hanging from, *de-pendere*. (No accident, perhaps, that this is exactly what Marden's linear networks often do, stretch towards one another and hang from the top edge of the canvas.) And in both cases, whether attendant or *attendant*, following or waiting, there is a temporality at play that resists the fixation of a noun, of a figure.

But here the similarity between attendant the adjective and *attendant* the participle stops, for a consequence always arrives (by definition) while something or someone awaited (like Godot) may not. It is the difference between logic and faith, rule and exception, the ironclad and the unknowable. And it is in this difference, this opposition, that we may find Marden's art.

Let us focus on the first of these two senses of 'attendant' – on logic, rules, or something closely related, the automatic. (What is entailed by logic or a rule follows, as we say, automatically.) For 'automatic' is the word that Marden more often uses when talking about his art, or at least about his drawing process:

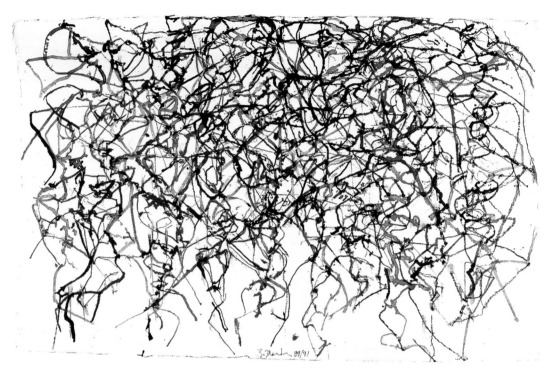

Brice Marden
St. Barts 12
1989–91
Ink on handmade paper
27.3 × 40.3 cm
Collection David Geffen

I think the closest I ever get to any sort of meditative state is when I'm drawing…
I start out, with a formal structure – couplets or whatever. Then I take it from there.
It's about joining things up, making relationships, but at the same time letting the
drawing itself do the work. One of the things about the work in this show is, it's
more directly involved in the act of drawing and the automatic. They start out with
observation and then automatic reaction, and then back off, so there's layering
of different ways of drawing.[7]

Here, talking about the drawings he made in 1986–91 following his discovery of Chinese
and Japanese calligraphy, Marden suggests a relationship between a 'formal structure' and a
desired state of automatism or meditativeness. The top-down, right-to-left order of a page of
calligraphy, often organised in couplets (paired columns), provides a structure within which he
can forget himself and let the drawing take over, so that in some way it will produce itself, 'do
the work'. The *fact* of a structure is more important than the particular structure itself: 'couplets
or whatever'. The important thing is to have a motivation, a motif, an object of 'observation'
as a starting point. In the case of the twelve *St. Barts* drawings (1989–91), the motif is, as
Marden reports in the same interview, both 'a palm grove that I worked in' (he always speaks
of working 'in' rather than 'on' a motif) and a structure of vertical couplets, ranging from two

to five in number. The most exciting drawings are those Marden has placed at the end of the series (nos. 10–12), where the tangle of the couplets and the tangle of the palm grove seem to grow together.

Of course, the idea of a self-generating drawing is something of a fiction. And it is even further out of reach in the more anxious, ambitious realm of painting. Yet it was the goal Marden set himself in the six *Cold Mountain* paintings of 1988–91, the second of which is exhibited here. These constitute the peak of his engagement with a quasi-calligraphic procedure:

> One of the things I wanted to do in the *Cold Mountain* paintings was to lose myself in the same way that I lose myself when I am drawing. A drawing is not terribly threatening… Because of that freedom from concern, the decisions can be more automatic, more gestural, less thought out, and that's when drawing, for me, becomes a meditative state. I have not been able to achieve that state when I paint because every decision is considered… But when I started the paintings, there were so many things that startled me. I was just astonished to find out that despite all the preparation, I still just had to start the painting. It was automatic; it was gestural and automatic. And I just had to try to lose myself again.[8]

Here Marden describes the facilitating ground of the automatic differently: not structure or motif but gesture ('gestural and automatic'). And yet by gesture he does not mean a physical fluidity or psychological directness of mark-making, which is the usual sense, but rather the habitual movements of the body when confronted with the blank canvas: 'I still just had to start the painting.'

One physical habit in play, especially at the start of the painting, is the artist's left-handedness: 'I usually just walk up and spontaneously start, which results in a certain left-handedness; there's a predictable way something will happen on one side, as opposed to the other side.'[9] Brenda Richardson, observing Marden at work, notes that he is to some extent ambidextrous but 'clearly favors his left hand for the decisive brushstroke'.[10] Marden was discouraged by the (false) idea that calligraphy must be learned with the right hand.[11] But, while he never learned calligraphy, he soon realised that imitating the right-to-left flow of characters on the page meant that 'I don't run the chance of smudging the ink or some marking.'[12] Whether Marden's left-handedness is present in the finished work, not just in the starting attack, is hard to say; but it is worth noting that in all the *Attendants* the shapes made by the dominant colours tend to be anchored at bottom right and to rise and expand toward the top left, resulting in a right-left movement for the whole shape that is the opposite of what occurs in most Western figurative compositions.[13]

Other physical constraints, it should be noted, may be self-imposed: 'A good way to approach a painting is to look at it from a distance roughly equivalent to its height, then double that distance, then go back and look at it in detail where you can begin to answer the questions you've posed at each of these various viewing distances.'[14] Presumably Marden has employed this viewing protocol not just in museums and galleries but in his own studio as he works and revises. At times Marden has used an equally choreographed protocol for the act of painting. In 1973 he reported: 'I work from panel to panel. I will paint on one until I arrive at a colour that holds that plane. I move to another panel and paint until something is holding that plane that also interestingly relates to the other panels. I work the third, searching for a colour value that pulls the planes together into a plane that has aesthetic meaning.'[15]

Unlike the Surrealists, then, who tried in their *écriture automatique* for a direct dictation from the unconscious, a stenography freed of all censorship or hindrance, Marden's concept of 'automatic' artistic production is bound up with self-imposed rules (e.g. 'I will compose the image in vertical columns' or 'I will work from panel to panel') and physical habits (e.g. left-handedness). But the goal of all this is not so different from that of the Surrealists. Marden's rules and constraints allow him to think less about certain aspects of his practice, and thus to be (as Jackson Pollock liked to say) 'in' the painting rather than apart from it; to be, at least part of the time, less self-conscious and more unconscious.

This is very much the sense of 'automatism' proposed by the American philosopher Stanley Cavell, who defines the task of the modern artist as that of finding over and over again 'a new automatism'.[16] By 'automatism' Cavell means 'both the broad genres or forms in which an art organizes itself (e.g., the fugue, the dance forms, blues) and those local events or *topoi* around which a genre precipitates itself (e.g., modulations, inversions, cadences).' These forms and devices offer the artist a structure within which he can let go, experiencing a freedom that would not be possible without the dialectical counterweight of the new formal constraint.

The word 'automatism' is doubly appropriate for modernism, Cavell argues persuasively. First, the discovery of a new automatism, be it a whole new form or simply a new kind of device, often generates 'further instances' of itself, and it seems to do so automatically (here Cavell cites the importance of the series). As Marden says, 'I always have this feeling more and more, that I can just go on and on and on and on.'[17] Second, the modern artist often experiences good work as 'happening of itself', and thus – using a more venerable term in the modernist lexicon – 'autonomous'. Here Cavell might have quoted Picasso, who proclaimed in 1923 (insisting significantly on the passive voice, as if there were no maker), 'When a form is realised, it is there to live its own life.'[18] Marden would certainly agree: 'One of the purposes of making a painting is knowing that... it will live not for thirty years but for thirty thousand years.'[19]

What are the new automatisms proposed by the *Attendants*? It is not enough to say, as I did earlier, that the 'looping patterns are clearer than ever, and the different colours of line easier to distinguish.' To qualify as an automatism, not just a style or manner, this greater clarity must rise to the level of a procedure or rule. In the *Attendants*, Marden has for the first time consistently maintained a system of apparent layering throughout a body of work, a system in which a line

Brice Marden
Little Red Painting
1994
Oil on linen
60.9 × 45.8 cm
Collection Susan and David Gersh

of one colour always lies on top of a line of another colour, or to put it more exactly, always behaves the same way at its intersection with another. In the first painting in the series, simply titled *Attendant*, the pale orange always takes precedence when it meets the pale green, interrupting it and thus appearing to lie on top of it. In *Attendant 2*, the layering (from the 'top' down) goes red/blue/salmon; in *Attendant 3*, orange/light blue/dark blue; and so on.[20] How different from such earlier works included here as *Kalo Keri* (1990), *Presentation* (1990–92) or *The Sisters* (1991–93), where no system of layers is present – where if red crosses yellow in one place, yellow crosses red (or yellow crosses blue, which in turn crosses red) in another. In these works we should speak rather of a braiding, albeit somewhat loosely, for there is no regular system of interlacing, as in the braiding of hair or rope.

The kind of regular 'layering' in the *Attendants* (the quotes indicate that it is a spatial illusion, not a matter of one pigment actually laid over another) is not new in Marden's work. Writing about *Little Red Painting* (1994), Charles Wylie notes a similar layering: 'the red and the yellow form interlock in a tight embrace, the red form remaining behind the yellow.'[21] But that small painting was exceptional, and not, as Wylie suggests, 'a concise example of Marden's language' in the other works from the time, the nine paintings of 1993–95 shown at Matthew

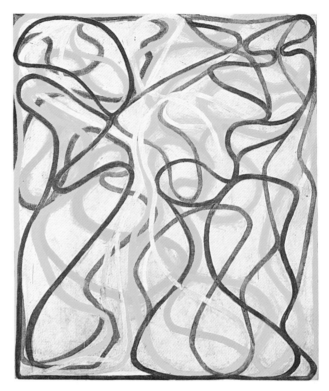

Brice Marden
Calcium
1993–95
Oil on linen
180.3 × 134.6 cm
Private collection

Marks Gallery in 1995–96. True, in *Daoist Portrait* the layering is consistent: light blue/dark brown/orange–yellow/light brown. But in *Calcium* the green and the brighter yellow follow each other closely, trading positions several times in the sandwich; and in *Skull with Thought* the light blue winds 'over' and 'under' the ochre. In *Light in the Forest* there is a consistent layering, but (for reasons discussed below) it is very hard to determine.

In Marden's next set, the 'Chinese work' (eight paintings of 1993–97), the layering is generally more candid and more consistent. In *Tang Dancer* (not an easy one to figure out) the order is dark blue/yellow/light blue/green/red; in *Suzhou* (an easier one) it is grey/blue/green; in *Epitaph Painting 1* it is black/yellow/blue (with one exception, black under yellow at upper right); and in *China Painting* it is yellow/green/dark blue. But in this last one there is a wild card, a light blue that lies under all the colours in some places and over all of them in others, most noticeably where it makes a little loop just below centre at left. And in *Chinese Dancing* and *Epitaph Painting 2* there is no system at all. Along the left edge of *Chinese Dancing* there is, in fact, a tight braiding of red and orange-yellow.[22]

This brings us back up to the present, to the *Attendants*, where the layering is maintained without exception. What are we to make of this? For one thing, it is a rejection of an important

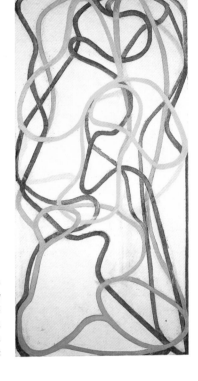

Brice Marden
Suzhou
1995–96
Oil on linen
180.3 × 83.3 cm
Private collection
Courtesy
Thomas Ammann
Fine Art, Zurich

Brice Marden
China Painting
1995–96
Oil on linen
180.3 × 243.8 cm
Collection of the artist

model. Yve-Alain Bois has pointed out the relevance to Marden of Mondrian's colour-stripe paintings of 1941–42, the so-called 'New York City' series (named after the finished painting of the set, the one that Mondrian translated from its working state of coloured adhesive tapes into oil paint). Comparing Mondrian's unfinished *New York City II* to Marden's *Presentation* (1990–92), Bois notes that while Marden's obsessive scraping is the opposite of Mondrian's physical layering of tape, 'the sense of a fleeting articulation in depth, always contradicted, always abolished as soon as it is grasped, is similar.'[24] And this deliberately unsystematic braiding, Bois has shown elsewhere, was something Mondrian deliberately found in *New York City*. Closely comparing the finished work to a photograph of the work in progress, Bois observes: 'of the six exceptions to the global system of coloured superimposition in the finished painting, only one… is visible in the photo of this stage of the work.'[25]

In the *Attendants*, Marden has effectively reversed the process by which Mondrian produced *New York City*, returning from exception to rule. In so doing, he seems to be returning to a mode he proposed in several canvases of 1987–88. While these paintings are not included here, they are nonetheless important to mention briefly, for in fact they are quite different, and the difference is telling.

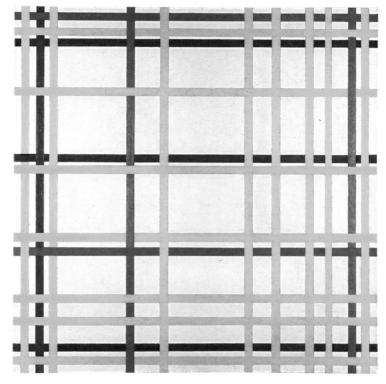

Piet Mondrian
New York City I
1942
Oil on canvas
119 × 114 cm
Collections Mnam/Cci –
Centre Georges Pompidou

In these earlier works, Bois notes, Marden 'made absolutely certain that the position of the layers in space remains constant, that there would be no contradiction in their overlappings'[26] (just as in the *Attendants*). But there were other contradictions: 'the artist experimented for the first time with the notion... that what comes after should look as if painted "before" (the simplest case is given by the energetic *11 (to Léger)* [1987–88], where the strokes of the red web patently interrupt their course to give way to those of the black mesh, except for two or three exceptions not so easily detected).'[27] In other words, the red line seems to lie underneath the black because it stops whenever it reaches the black and then continues on the other side, giving the sense that the black has come over the red and temporarily hidden it; and yet the *way* that the red line stops, thickening just as it reaches the black (as the brush slows to a halt), reveals that it has been applied after the black. To put it simply, 'under' comes after and 'over' comes before. And this is hard to swallow since we normally expect 'under' to equal before and 'over' to equal after, especially in a painting as direct and gestural, as indexical of the artist's process, as *11 (to Léger)* is – or at first appears to be.

Thus the rigidity of the apparent layering in Marden's 1987–88 works, the suppression of braiding, was in the service of a higher-order braiding, of under/over with before/after, of

Brice Marden
11 (to Leger)
1987–88
Oil on linen
213.3 × 152.4
Collection Linda and Harry Macklowe, New York

space with time: 'the temporal and the spatial orders contradict one another: this provokes a spiraling effect, a to and fro, that is visually uncontrollable.'[28] In the *Attendants*, on the other hand, such higher-order confusion is rarely present. Only occasionally does an 'underlying' line obviously interrupt itself to avoid crossing one already in place.

The regularity of the *Attendants* is nicely thrown into relief by Marden's four recently completed *Sepia Drawings* involving black, white and red, and all included here. Each of these contains one aggressive exception to a layering rule: *1* is black over white over red except for an emphatic moment to the right of centre where red crosses white just when both lines are at their thickest; *2* is black over red over white except where white takes a dramatic turn at upper left, parting from the black line it has been doubling in order to cut through red; and *3* is also black over red over white, but this time red cuts through black at middle left just at the confluence of three black lines.[29] In each case, Marden locates this spatial and logical knot at a point of great linear activity, creating the sense that the drawing produces itself as it slowly untangles itself from that point.

What has Marden gained by his thoroughgoing systematisation in the *Attendants*? One obvious answer might be: a greater automatism, a more rigorous application of a procedure or rule. Keeping the apparent layers constant means the artist has one less thing to think about. But if we recall that the point of Marden's automatism is, as he said, 'to lose myself', to let the painting 'do the work', then the *Attendants* are also *less* automatic because they are less tangling of the beholder's perception than are any of the earlier, braided works. They do not lose us, or presumably the artist, in themselves; they do not take over. The mode of beholding required by *Kalo Keri* (1990) and so nicely described by Bois – 'you do not attempt to disentangle the snarls any more, you give it up, you willingly become short-sighted, satisfied only to arrest your eyes on this or that part of the evermoving maze'[30] – is forsworn, and with it, perhaps, the trancelike state Marden seeks. This would be a loss, not a gain.

Maybe what Marden gains is a sense of time. The illusion of layers in the *Attendants* offers an archaeological dimension that is absent from the braided works. The process of layering, the creation of a palimpsest, has always been important to Marden, especially in his 'work book' drawings, those that he carries with him from place to place and returns to again and again.[31] (Recall too the passage cited earlier, where he speaks of a 'layering of different ways of drawing'.) But while in his drawings Marden's use of white gouache as an eraser preserves to some extent the visibility of what is underneath, the paintings usually involve too much scraping down and backtracking to offer a temporal trace of their own making. Perhaps the recovery of this kind of trace of before and after, if only as an illusion, is one of Marden's goals in embracing a 'layering' in the *Attendants*.

But that seems too elaborate. Maybe Marden has gained something much simpler: the Figure, or at least the Shape or Gestalt (the very thing that Mondrian's braiding sought to destroy). Free of entanglements, we experience each colour in the *Attendants* separately, as a closed linear network consisting of an external contour and several internal contours, or, to put it another way, as a self-contained jigsaw puzzle. In *Attendant*, for example, the pale orange circuit has five pieces, the pale green one two; in *Attendant 4 (Monk)*, the red-orange circuit has five pieces, the green one four.

But this flattened reading breaks down almost as soon as it starts, for two reasons. First of all, the contours of any given colour are arranged in such a way that the distinction between external and internal contour is blurred. As lines of the same colour converge and diverge, we begin to read a three-dimensional tracery, a play of lassos, a drawing in space where crossing is not necessarily meeting – or else a schematic, outlined rendering of the differently angled planes of a solid (as in Dubuffet's well-known post-1962 style of painting and sculpture, which he nicknamed 'l'Hourloupe'). Secondly, not all the networks are closed: the dark blue in *Attendant 2* simply ends at the bottom right corner, leaving us unsure if the shape it cuts out in the lower right quadrant is 'its' or not. In *Attendant 3*, we complete the dark blue circuit by inferring its continuation at various points along all the edges of the canvas (and in parts of the centre too), where, we tell ourselves, it is 'hidden beneath' the other colours.[32] In *Attendant 5*, this

Jean Dubuffet
Passe cortège
12 octobre 1965
Oil on canvas
97 × 130 cm
Courtesy
Waddington Galleries,
London

work of interpolation must be done dramatically across the upper centre, where to complete the yellow circuit we attempt to imagine a yellow underpass beneath the red. Probably the hardest such interpolation is posed by the oft-interrupted salmon-coloured line in *Attendant 2*, where the difficulty seems to issue in unusual pools of that colour at the top right and along the left edge.

All of which is to say that in their apparent simplicity, the *Attendants* stimulate our figurative appetite only to frustrate it. The braiding of differently coloured lines, of before/after and over/under, of space and time, is gone; in its place, however, is the braiding of positive and negative space, line and shape, figure and ground, open and closed form.

I suspect that Marden has gained something more basic from the systematisation in the *Attendants*, something self-conscious and retrospective. In their candidness and clarity, these pictures allow us to make sense of the tangled viewing that Marden's networks have demanded for over a decade.

Let us step back from the mad pursuit of lines that has been absorbing us and consider briefly just how it is we have been determining the sequences of layers. Take *Attendant 2* as

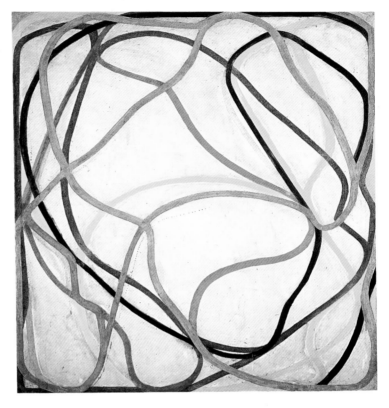

Brice Marden
Light in the Forest
1993–95
Oil on canvas
180.3 × 144.8 cm
Collection
Frances and John Bowes

a case in point. One way is too look for intersections of different-coloured lines in order to get a rapid reading of the colour-space configuration at a given point. Since there are three colours, look for three-way interchanges, for example, just above and to the left of centre (red-blue-pink), and then quickly check other such intersections for confirmation or denial. (By intersection I do not necessarily mean a place where the three lines meet exactly and cross all at once, for there the apparent under-over relations may well be obscured, but rather a place where each of the three lines crosses another in close proximity.) The other way is to choose the colour that seems most to lie on top and quickly follow it round, making sure that it is always crossing, never crossed; and then proceed to the presumptive next layer, and so on. For some paintings, the first method works better; for others, the second. (In fact, this is one way to classify Marden's paintings.)

Take *Light in the Forest* (1993 – 95). Our eye is immediately attracted by the many nodes in the multicoloured linear network, but none of them offers the explication of layers we wish. At the bottom-centre juncture of red with black and two shades of grey, for example, we learn only that the light grey lies on top, and nothing about the mutual relations of the other three colours. The same thing happens time and again, until we realise that we would do much better to follow the lines in their courses, for the overlapping information is contained not at the nodes but rather at the more haphazard crossings of one line with another. And so the investigation begins. In this way Marden instructs our viewing, enforcing a circuitous method as if to teach us to give every part of the canvas its due. 'I tend to follow the lines, and in a way it's like a journey,' Marden has said.[33]

In *Tang Dancer* (1995–96), on the other hand, the entire system can be grasped by looking at one of any number of small areas with a lot of crossings. We solve the problem quickly, and the reward is that our gaze is free to relax and wander, which seems appropriate to the linear shapes that twist extravagantly around the work's grey-blue spine. This is the opposite of the intense, searching tour enforced by *Light in the Forest*. Which is not to say that *Tang Dancer* is worse or better, only that (for all its similarity) it is completely different.

In his perceptive essay on Marden's 'Chinese work', Jonathan Hay finds 'a tremendous clarity that functions at both local and general levels of the picture surface with almost precisely the same demand on the eye, so that there is a constant oscillation between the two'. This distinction between local and general levels of the surface parallels the one I have drawn between local (*Tang Dancer*) and general (*Light in the Forest*) modes of viewing, between looking at nodes and following paths. Except, as we have just seen, the demand within any given work is not usually equal. What distinguishes the *Attendants* from Marden's other work, in fact, is that both the general and local methods *do* work equally well (as we saw in *Attendant 2*: I leave it to the reader to confirm this in the others). Which is why the *Attendants* serve as a kind of key to the viewing of Marden's work of the 1990s.

The resulting equipoise of the *Attendants* – the balance of local and general viewing that they solicit – brings them structurally close to what the American cognitive scientist Douglas Hofstadter, writing in *Gödel, Escher, Bach: An Eternal Golden Braid*, calls a semantic network. Hofstadter describes this mapping of conceptual connections within a mind or thought process or computer as follows: 'Suppose we now agree that there are certain drawings of nodes, connected by links (let us say they come in various colours, so that various types of conceptual nearness can be distinguished from each other), which capture precisely the way in which symbols trigger other symbols.' The resulting coloured web has both local and global (what I am calling local and general) properties. 'Local properties require only a very nearsighted observer – for example an observer who can only see one vertex at a time; and global properties require only a sweeping vision, without attention to detail.' Then there is the question of 'which kind of observation' is a 'more reliable guide' in characterising the basic structure of the network, in determining whether it is 'isomorphic' with another network, and so on.[34]

Of course, Marden's paintings are not actual semantic networks: they do not illustrate a set of conceptual connections. But their similarity to Hofstadter's imagined map of such a network is not accidental, for the *Attendants* engage us in a compelling map-reading process that is at once conceptual, visual and virtually physical.

To see it another way, what we have in Marden's paintings, whether of the braided or layered type, is (following Hofstadter, and recalling Cavell above) a kind of fugue. A fugue, to over-

Frantisek Kupka
Amorpha:
Fugue in Two Colours
1912
Oil on canvas
211 × 220 cm
National Gallery, Prague

simplify, is a polyphonic musical composition in which two or more distinct voices or melodic lines are introduced sequentially and arranged so that they seem to flee (Latin: *fugere*) from one another or pursue one another (a closely related term, often synonymous with fugue, is the Italian *ricercare*, to search). What facilitates the mesmerising chase is the fact that the distinct lines share similar rhythmic motifs and are composed in counterpoint (related through a variety of inversions and variations), even when they are improvised.[35]

'One of the reasons I wanted to do this work,' Marden has said of his post-1985 production, 'was that by using the monochromatic palette in the past basically all I could get were chords. I wanted to be able to make something more like fugues, more complicated, back-and-forth renderings of feelings.'[36] Here Marden joins a long list of modern painters (Kupka, Klee, Mondrian, van Doesburg, Schwitters and Robert Delaunay, to name a few) for whom Bach and especially his fugues were a privileged model of non-referential art, proof that a formal structure could replace an observed object as the motif or *raison d'être* of a painting. Kupka stated in 1913: 'I am still fumbling in the dark but I think I can find something between sight and hearing and that I can produce a fugue in colours like Bach has done in music.'[37]

Of course, each of these artists used the model differently. Perhaps the most literal of them

Jacopo da Pontormo
Deposition
c. 1526 – 28
Oil on wood
313 × 192 cm
S. Felicita, Florence

was van Doesburg, whose stained-glass and mosaic works of the teens were based on symmetrical reflections and inversions. Marden considers the fugue less literally but not, perhaps, less seriously. What makes the *Attendants* fugal is that in each one the different colours of line have enough in common – width, scraped texture, degree of curviness, number of branchings, saturation of colour – to make them close variations on one another; and this closeness is thematised, as it were, in the way that they stay away from one another in some places only to join up in others. To put it simply, Marden seems to have grasped the paradox at the heart of the fugue: the more similar the various voices in the polyphony (or polychromy), the more potentially complex their interplay.

This gives the paintings a temporal dimension, even if it is not the linear temporality of music. Marden's just-quoted statement indicates that what the linear networks offered him was not simply a range of colour notes (for that was fully present in his multi-panel monochrome paintings of the sixties and seventies) but their distension and entwining. He moved from simultaneity to temporality, from 'chords' to 'back-and-forth renderings'. And not just back and forth but also circling and circulating. Perhaps the best way to describe the movement in time generated by Marden's paintings of the past decade is simply to recall Sydney Freedberg's memorable account of Jacopo Pontormo's *Deposition* (*c.*1526–28): 'It moves in a counterclockwise interlacing like a visual polyphony, unfolding the narrative and commenting on its emotions as it proceeds... There is no end to the movement of this circular polyphony and no release from it except by the spectator's act of will.'[38] So too with Marden's paintings: the mutual entanglement of forms implicates us as well, and we find ourselves hard-pressed to escape from the 'cursive connexion among shapes that binds them in melodic unity'.[39]

But there is an escape (other than looking away). Sometimes, when things are going well, the play of pursuit and flight (*ricercare/fugere*) delivers us to another level of response. What Marden has said about how he approaches Pollock's *White Light* (1954) can be read as a hint about where our viewing of his works should arrive:

> When you read the levels of *White Light*, you start from the ground – the canvas –
> and then you read the blue, the yellow, to the red, then the whites, then you see
> the blacks going through, then the blues, and suddenly, if you're responding,
> you enter a world that is really inexplicable.[40]

This is the end of rules, both their purpose and their terminus. Marden's constantly mutating procedures for painting and protocols for viewing are meant only to create the conditions for their own irrelevance. 'The paintings are made in a highly subjective state within Spartan limitations.'[41] 'You make up a set of rules, but you don't have to adhere to them.'[42] 'One of the things that art does is, lead you to forget the rules.'[43] Here Marden's automatism rejoins that of the Surrealists – on the ground of the irrational, or at least unexpectable. Rosalind Krauss, revisiting Cavell, writes, 'What "automatism" thrusts into the foreground... is the concept of improvisation, of the need to take chances in the face of a medium now cut free from the guarantees of artistic tradition. It is this sense of the improvisatory that welcomes the word's associations with "psychic automatism".'[44] In Marden's recent work, as in musical improvisation, the rules and constraints are there to summon moments of unruly inspiration, of afflatus (from the Latin *afflare*, to breathe on). Except that such moments cannot be summoned, only set up.

Here we should recall that other meaning of 'attendant', the participle squeezed earlier from the French: waiting (for the muses, the inexplicable, 'the all'[45]). Perhaps there is a noun at play too, a reference to Marden's days as a uniformed attendant at the Jewish Museum in New York, where he must have learned how to slow the pace of vision, how to wait. Perhaps the titles of Marden's new paintings are simply saying *wait and see*.

Notes

My thanks to Sarah Boxer, Lisa Corrin, Leigh Markopoulos, Yve-Alain Bois and Linda Norden
for their valuable editorial suggestions.

1
Marden, conversation with Charles Wylie, 6 July 1998, referring
to *Study for the Muses (Eaglesmere Version)*, cited in Wylie,
'A Spartan Humanism: Brice Marden's Work of the 1990s', in
Brice Marden, Work of the 1990s: Paintings, Drawings, and Prints,
exh. cat. (Dallas Museum of Art and others, 1999 – 2000), p. 62.

2
Marden, interview with Jonathan Hay, in *Brice Marden: Chinese
Work*, exh. cat. (Matthew Marks Gallery, 1997), p. 30.

3
Marden, conversation with Brenda Richardson, 1989 – 91, cited
in Richardson, 'The Way to Cold Mountain', in *Brice Marden:
Cold Mountain*, exh. cat. (Dia Center for the Arts and others,
1991 – 92), p. 57.

4
Marden, interview with Janie C. Lee, 21 May 1998, referring
to the Cold Mountain drawings, in *Brice Marden Drawings:
The Whitney Museum of American Art Collection*, exh. cat. (Whitney Museum of American Art, 1998 – 99), p. 22.

5
Marden, interview with Hay, p. 30. Perhaps the simple-mindedness
of this dictum, and the fact that Marden has done few square
paintings, should make us sceptical of it.

6
Marden, interview with Hay, p. 30.

7
Marden, interview with Pat Steir, in *Brice Marden: Recent Drawings
and Etchings*, exh. cat. (Matthew Marks, 1991), n.p.

8
Marden, cited in Richardson, 'The Way', p. 70.

9
Marden, interview with Hay, p. 21.

10
Richardson, 'The Way', p. 68.

11
Ibid., n.p.

12
Marden, interview with Lee, p. 19.

13
The standard presentation of the Annunciation, for example, is
from left to right, although the 'Annunciation from the right' forms
an interesting sub-genre.

14
Marden, cited in Richardson, 'The Way', p. 43. See also Marden's comment in the interview with Hay (p. 20) about his studio
practice: 'You're working from a distance, and then you're working very close up.'

15
From Brice Marden, 'Statements, Notes, and Interviews' (1963 – 81),
in *Brice Marden: Paintings, Drawings and Prints 1975 – 1980*,
exh. cat. (Whitechapel Gallery, 1981), pp. 54 – 57, reprinted
in Kristine Stiles and Peter Selz, eds, *Theories and Documents
of Contemporary Art: A Sourcebook of Artists' Writings*
(Berkeley: University of California Press, 1996), p. 139. I do
not know whether Marden still employs such procedures.

16
Stanley Cavell, *The World Viewed: Reflections on the Ontology
of Film* (New York: Viking, 1971), pp. 101 – 08.

17
Marden, interview with Pat Steir, n.p.

18
Pablo Picasso, 'Statement to Marius de Zayas, 1923', in Edward
R. Fry, *Cubism* (New York: Oxford University Press, 1966), p. 167.

19
Marden, cited in Richardson, 'The Way', pp. 74 – 75.

20
I was not able to see a reproduction of *Attended 6* before writing.
[Subsequent to the completion of this essay the artist renamed
this painting *The Attended*. Ed.]

21
Interesting that Wylie speaks of a 'tight embrace' even as he is
observing the spatial non-interlacing of the two colours. Presumably
he is noting the pretzel-like surface pattern created by the two
forms. But I also take his observation as evidence of our desire
or nostalgia for the illusionistic spatial weave that Marden's work
since 1994 has increasingly refused.

22
Scott Rothkopf has identified a similar braiding (as well as its
de-figurative effect) in Miró's *Painting* (1953): 'Miró complicates
this gathering [of figures] by making his thick muscular lines playfully
slide over and under one another… On the tall central figure, one
apparently continuous mark defines the beak and most of the head.
It crosses the trunk or neck twice, slipping below the vertical line
at one point and crossing over it at another. Of course, it would
be physically impossible for two continuous lines to weave over
and under each other in this way. Miró's carefully constructed
illusion reinforces the nebulous, open effect of his figures, which
are as difficult to understand spatially as they are to identify
zoologically.' From *Modern Art at Harvard*, exh. cat. (The
Bunkamura Museum of Art and others, 1999 – 2000), p. 224.

23
This is a painting Marden has surely seen many times at the Kunststammlung Nordrhein-Westfalen in Dusseldorf, where we know he admires Pollock's *Number 32*, 1950.

24
Yve-Alain Bois, 'Marden's Doubt,' in *Brice Marden: Paintings 1985–1993*, exh. cat. (Kunsthalle Bern and Wiener Secession, 1993–94), p. 43.

25
Yve-Alain Bois, 'Piet Mondrian, *New York City*' (1985/88), in Bois, *Painting as Model* (Cambridge: MIT Press, 1990), p. 165.

26
Bois, 'Marden's Doubt', p. 45.

27
Likewise, in *The Studio* (1990), as Bois notes, the darker grey-blue tangle has been clearly painted after but appears under (because it is interrupted by) the dark green tangle. In *Diagrammed Couplet I* (1988–89) Bois finds a similar contradiction although (it should be noted) its operation is different: the paler 'threads' connecting the darker 'glyphs' look farther away in space because of their paleness, but have obviously been painted second because of their clear status as dilute annotations. Bois, 'Marden's Doubt', pp. 35, 39. Bois (p. 47) goes on to note the return of spatial braiding in *Picasso's Skull* (1989–90) and the *Cold Mountain* paintings (1988–91). A confirmation of Marden's habit of applying apparently underlying layers later can be found by comparing earlier states of *Epitaph Painting 2* with the finished work: see *Brice Marden: Chinese Work*, p. 21.

28
Bois, 'Marden's Doubt', p. 35.

29
In *4*, a beautifully spare drawing whose crystalline geometries hark back to Marden's 'glyphs' of the late 1980s, there are only two colours, with black consistently over white. Here what is exceptional is the way that the forms are not closed: the black tracery is allowed to end, twice, in mid-canvas, as if in mid-thought.

30
Bois, 'Marden's Doubt', p. 47.

31
See *Brice Marden, Work Books 1964–1995*, exh. cat. (Staatliche Graphische Sammlung München, Kunstmuseum Winterthur, and Harvard University Art Museums, 1997–98), eds Dieter Schwarz and Michael Semff.

32
This comforting work is interrupted near the bottom of the left edge, where the dark-blue line seems to curve inward and end abruptly at the orange line that cuts it off (until we realise that this bit of dark blue could equally be a glimpse of the line as it continues straight down and around the corner to join itself again along the bottom edge).

33
Marden, referring to *Epitaph Painting 2*, interview with Hay, p. 23.

34
Douglas R. Hofstadter, *Gödel, Escher, Bach: An Eternal Golden Braid* (New York: Basic Books, 1979), pp. 371–72.

35
Of course, this description oversimplifies a long and complex history. See Alfred Mann's classic *The Study of Fugue* (New York: W.W. Norton, 1965).

36
Marden, interview with Steir, n.p.

37
Cited in Virginia Spate, *Orphism: The Evolution of Painting in Paris, 1910–1914* (New York: Oxford University Press, 1979), p. 130.

38
S.J. Freedberg, *Painting in Italy, 1500–1600* (Harmondsworth: Penguin Books, 1975), p. 188.

39
Ibid., p. 187.

40
He continues: 'Different movements work against each other and with each other, and this grayish white starts moving through the painting one way, the yellow starts moving through the painting another way... When I talk about the grayish white that runs up through *White Light*, I have to talk about what it is for me to be in that grayish-white place. As I was coming uptown to the museum this afternoon, there was the most beautiful light.' ˚Marden, from Richardson's transcript of his MoMA gallery talk of 16 November 1989, cited in Richardson, 'The Way,' pp. 43–44. For more on Marden's reading of Pollock, see Bois, 'Marden's Doubt.'

41
Marden in 1963, reprinted in Stiles and Selz, *Theories & Documents*, p. 138. The dialectic of rule and feeling, of the Apollonian and the Dionysian, is a familiar *topos* of modernism: see for example Michael Fried's remark about Kenneth Noland's 'search for a set of formal constraints in which Noland himself could believe and under which his feelings could find release.' Fried, *Three American Painters*, exh. cat. (Fogg Art Museum, 1965), p. 28.

42
Marden, interview with Hay, p. 23.

43
Marden, interview with Steir, n.p.

44
Rosalind Krauss, '*A Voyage on the North Sea*': Art in the Age of the Post-Medium Condition (London: Thames & Hudson, 1999), pp. 5–6.

45
From Marden's Grove Group Notebook (page inscribed 'Hydra Greece Summer 1974'), reproduced in *Brice Marden: The Grove Group*, exh. cat. (Gagosian Gallery, 1973), p. 25.

Works in the Exhibition

1.
Cold Mountain 2
1989–91
Oil on linen
274.6 × 366.4 cm
Hirshhorn Museum and Sculpture Garden,
Smithsonian Institution, The Holenia Purchase
Fund, in memory of Joseph H. Hirshhorn,
1992

2.
Kalo Keri 1990
Oil on linen
235 × 150 cm
Kunstmuseum Winterthur.
Anonymous gift, 1991

3.
Presentation 1990–92
Oil on linen
235.5 × 150 cm
Collection Patricia Phelps de Cisneros

4.
Corpus 1991–93
Oil on linen
180.3 × 144.8 cm
Froehlich Collection, Stuttgart

5.
Virgins 1991–93
Oil on linen
243.8 × 259 cm
Private collection

6.
The Sisters 1991–93
Oil on linen
213.3 × 149.9 cm
Private collection

7.
The Muses 1991–93
Oil on linen
274.5 × 458 cm
Daros Collection, Switzerland

8.
Study for The Muses (Eaglesmere Version)
1991–94 / 1997–99
Oil on linen
210.8 × 342.9 cm
Collection of the artist

9.
Sepia Drawing I 1991–2000
Sepia wash, sepia ink, Kremer white
shellac ink, Kremer red shellac ink
on 300 lb. Lanaquarelle paper
75.9 × 50.8 cm
Francesco and Alba Clemente

10.
Sepia Drawing II 1991–2000
Sepia wash, sepia ink, Kremer shellac
inks on 300 lb. Lanaquarelle paper
76 × 51.4 cm
Private collection

11.
Sepia Drawing III 1991–2000
Sepia wash, sepia ink, Kremer shellac inks
on 300 lb. Lanaquarelle paper
76 × 51.4 cm
Collection of Ninah and Michael Lynne

12.
Sepia Drawing IV 1991–2000
Sepia wash, sepia ink, Kremer white shellac
ink on 300 lb. Lanaquarelle paper
75.7 × 52 cm
Collection of the artist

13.
Untitled Figure Drawing I 1992
Ink on paper (T.H. Saunders)
37.8 × 19.7 cm
Melia Marden

14.
Venus #2 (Negril) 1992–93
Ink on paper
102.9 × 65.7 cm
Collection of the artist

15.
Solstice 1993
Ink and gouache on paper
102.9 × 66 cm
Helen Marden

16.
Work Book Hydra – New York 1993–94
Ink and gouache on handmade paper
32 sheets
34.5 × 23.8 cm
Private collection, Baltimore MD

17.
Daoist Portrait 1993–95
Oil on linen
180.3 × 134.6 cm
Private collection

18.
Skull with Thought 1993–95
Oil on linen
108.3 × 144.8 cm
Keith and Katherine Sachs

19.
Chinese Dancing 1993–96
Oil on canvas
155 × 274.3 cm
Collection PaineWebber Group, Inc.,
New York

20.
Attendant 1996–99
Oil on linen
208.3 × 144.8 cm
Helen Marden

21.
Attendant 2 1996–99
Oil on linen
208 × 145 cm
Dr Paul and Dorie Sternberg

22.
Attendant 3 1996–99
Oil on linen
208 × 145 cm
Private collection, Switzerland;
Courtesy Thomas Ammann Fine Art, Zurich

23.
Attendant 4 (Monk) 1996–99
Oil on linen
208 × 145 cm
Private collection,
Courtesy Thomas Ammann Fine Art, Zurich

24.
Attendant 5 1996–99
Oil on linen
208 × 145 cm
Private collection, Baltimore MD

25.
The Attended 1996–99
Oil on linen
208 × 145 cm
Collection of the artist

26.
Untitled Red and Green Drawing 2 1998
Hand applied wash ground and
Kremer inks on Lanaquarelle paper
51.1 × 76.2 cm
Paul F. Walter

27.
Untitled Red and Green Drawing 3 1998
Hand applied wash ground and Kremer inks
on Lanaquarelle paper
51.1 × 76.2 cm
Collection of the artist

28.
Untitled Red and Green Drawing 4 1998
Hand applied wash ground and
Kremer inks on Lanaquarelle paper
51.2 × 75 cm
Private collection

1.
Cold Mountain 2
1989–91
Oil on linen
274.6 × 366.4 cm
Hirshhorn Museum and Sculpture
Garden, Smithsonian Institution,
The Holenia Purchase Fund, in
memory of Joseph H. Hirshhorn, 1992

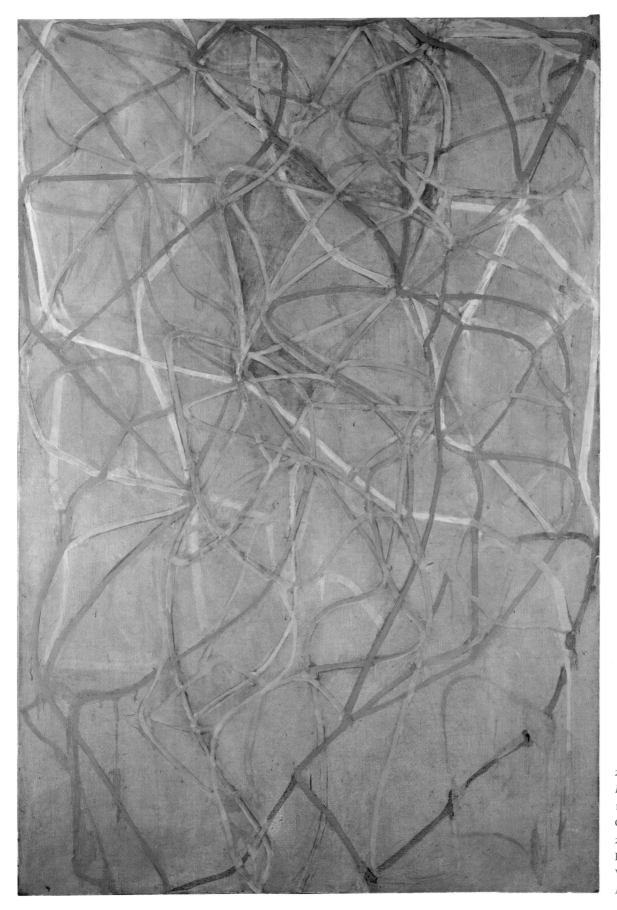

2.
Kalo Keri
1990
Oil on linen
235 × 150 cm
Kunstmuseum
Winterthur.
Anonymous gift, 1991

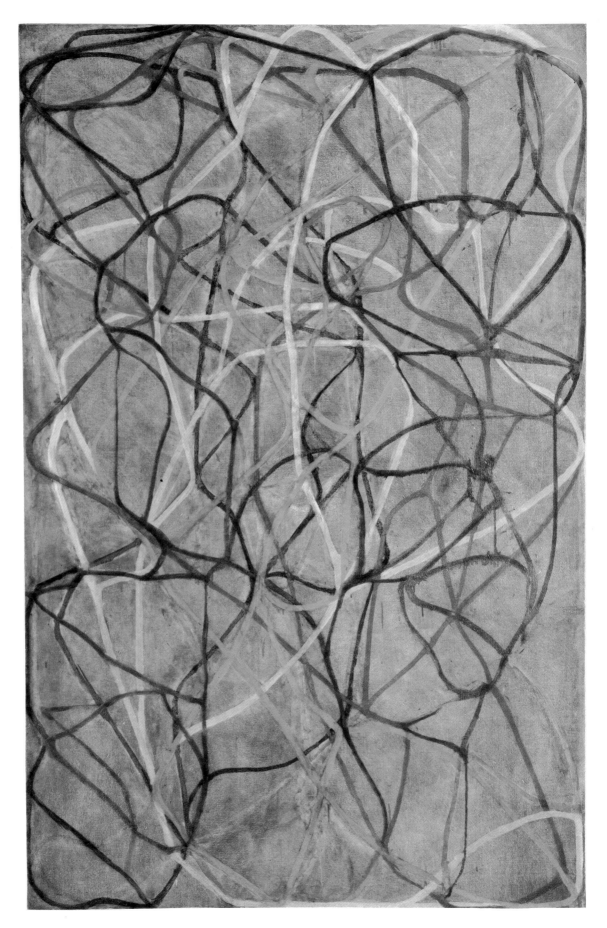

3.
Presentation
1990—92
Oil on linen
235.5 × 150 cm
Collection
Patricia Phelps de Cisneros

4.
Corpus
1991–93
Oil on linen
180.3 × 144.8 cm
Froehlich Collection, Stuttgart

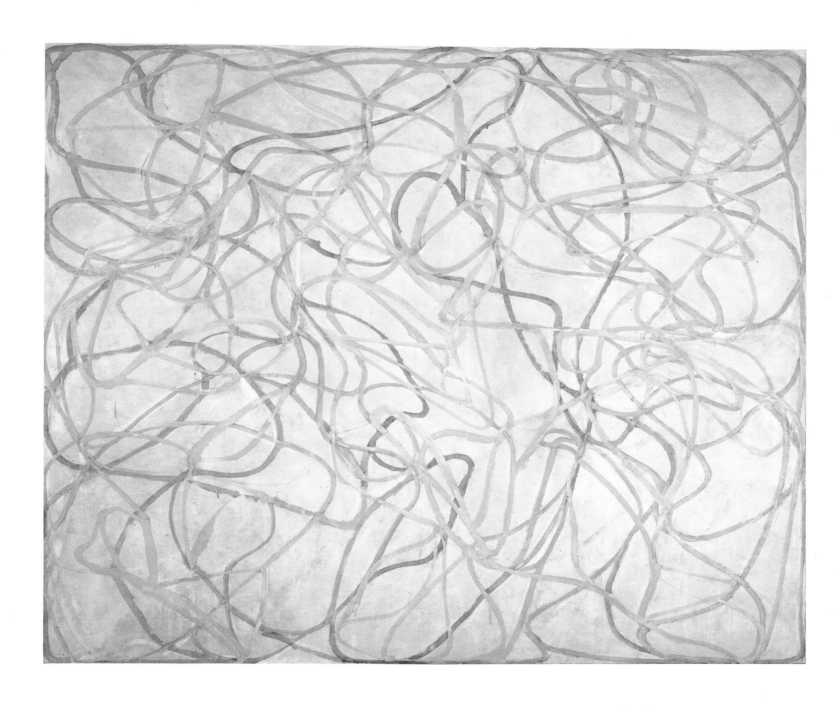

5.
Virgins
1991–93
Oil on linen
243.8 × 259 cm
Private collection

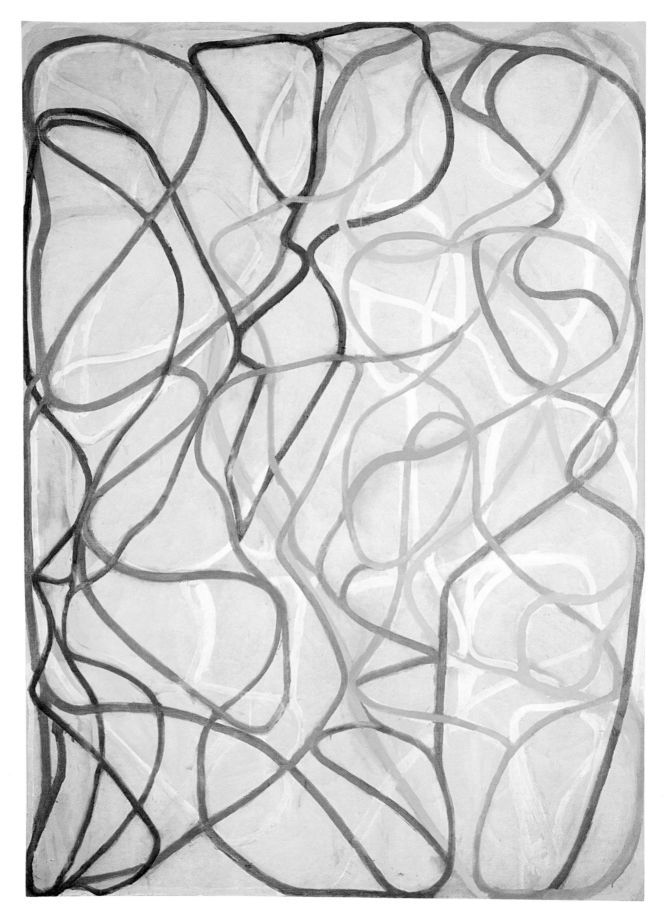

6.
The Sisters
1991–93
Oil on linen
213.3 × 149.9 cm
Private collection,
San Francisco

7.
The Muses
1991–93
Oil on linen
274.5 × 458 cm
Daros Collection,
Switzerland

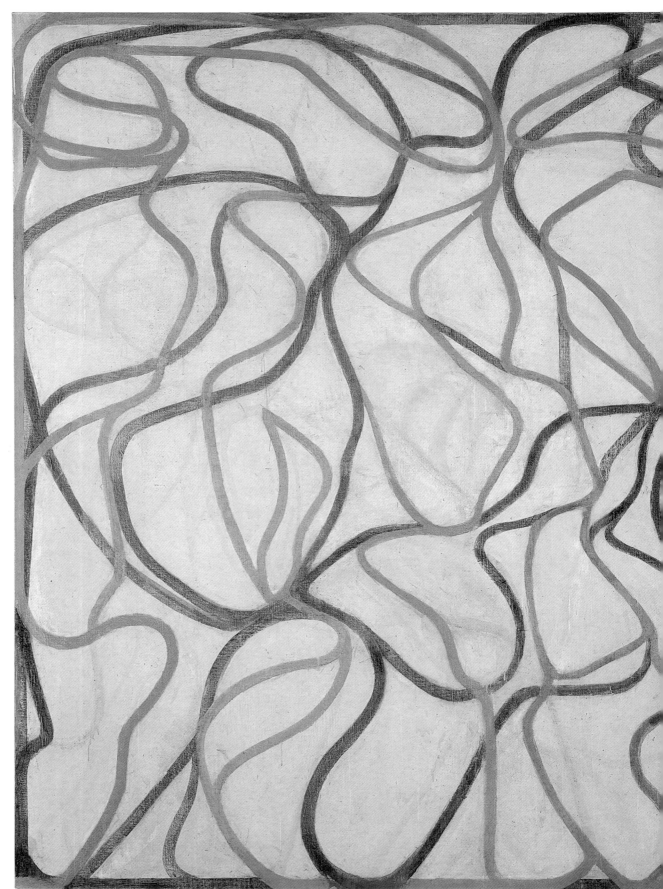

8.
*Study for The Muses
(Eaglesmere Version)*
1991−94/1997−99
Oil on linen
210.8 × 342.9 cm
Collection
of the artist

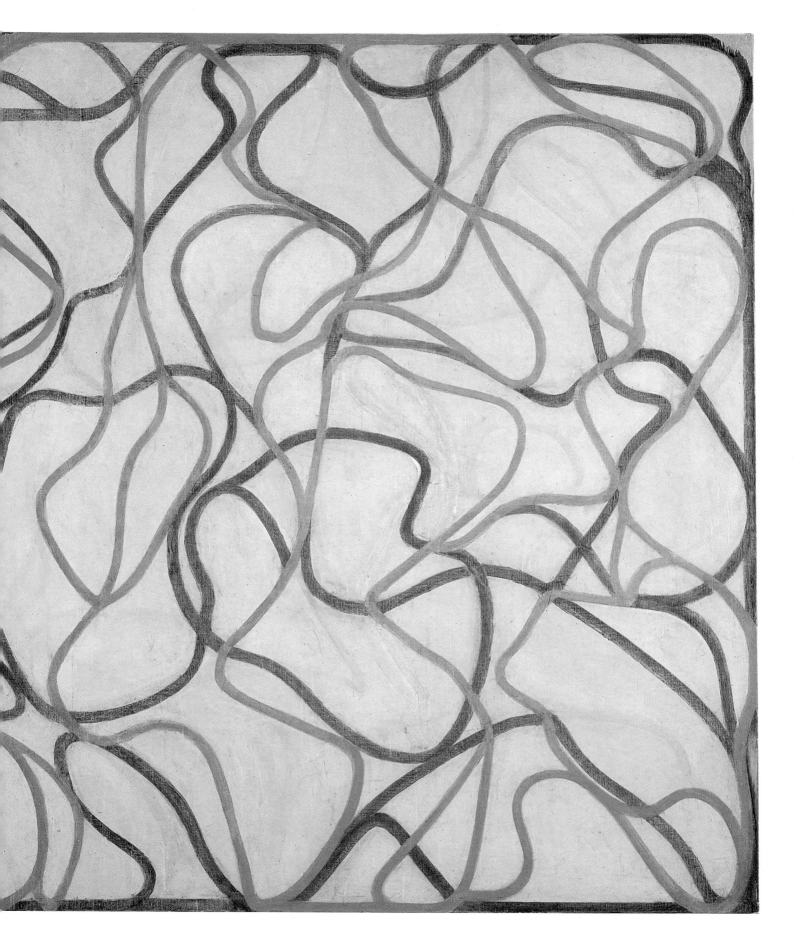

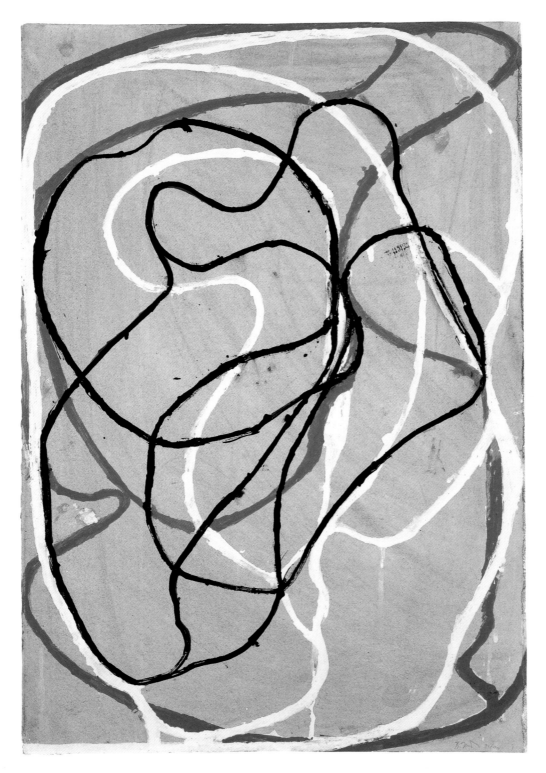

9.

Sepia Drawing I

1991–2000

Sepia wash, sepia ink, Kremer white shellac ink,

Kremer red shellac ink on 300 lb. Lanaquarelle paper

75.9 × 50.8 cm

Francesco and Alba Clemente

10.
Sepia Drawing II
1991 – 2000
Sepia wash, sepia ink, Kremer shellac inks on 300 lb.
Lanaquarelle paper
76 × 51.4 cm
Private collection

11.

Sepia Drawing III

1991 — 2000

Sepia wash, sepia ink, Kremer shellac inks on 300 lb.

Lanaquarelle paper

76 × 51.4 cm

Collection of Ninah and Michael Lynne

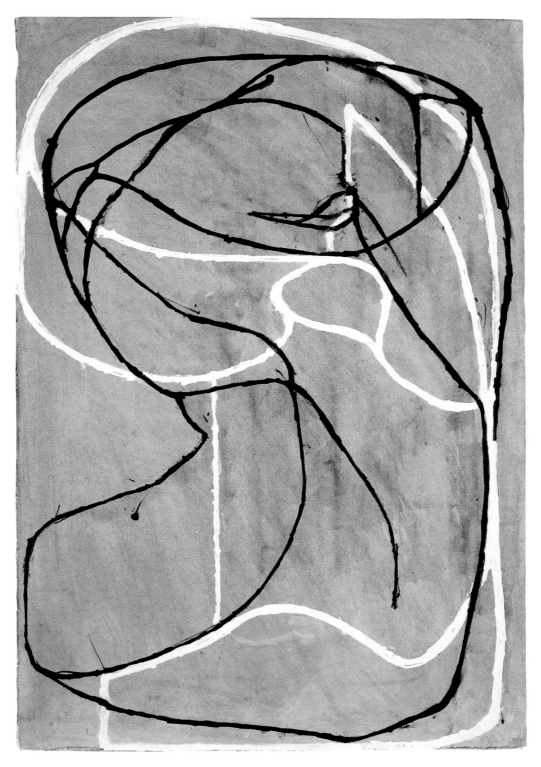

12.
Sepia Drawing IV
1991—2000
Sepia wash, sepia ink, Kremer white shellac ink on 300 lb.
Lanaquarelle paper
75.7 × 52 cm
Collection of the artist

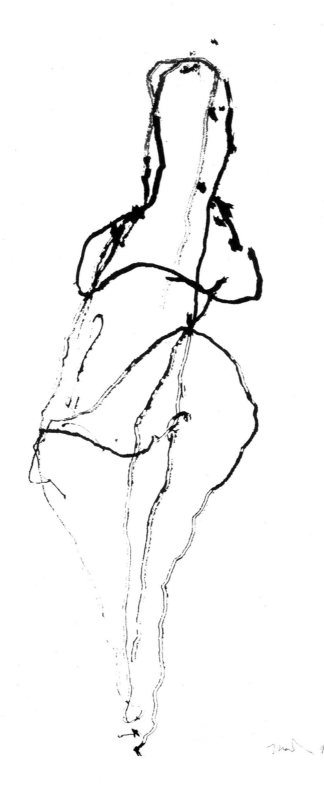

13.
Untitled Figure Drawing I
1992
Ink on paper (T.H. Saunders)
37.8 × 19.7 cm
Melia Marden

14.
Venus #2 (Negril)
1992–93
Ink on paper
102.9 × 65.7 cm
Collection of the artist

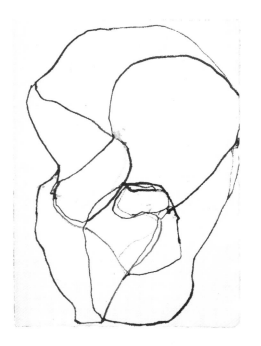

Work book, Hydra – New York
1993-94
32 sheets
B. Mord

16.
Work Book Hydra – New York
1993 – 94
Ink and gouache on handmade paper
32 sheets
34.5 × 23.8 cm
Private collection, Baltimore MD

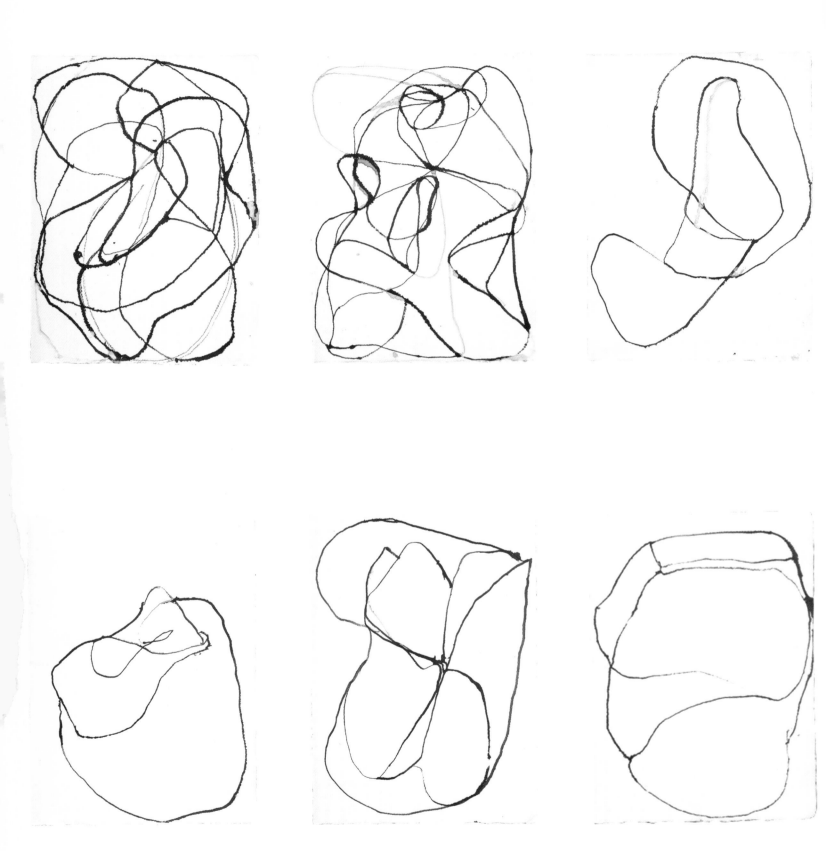

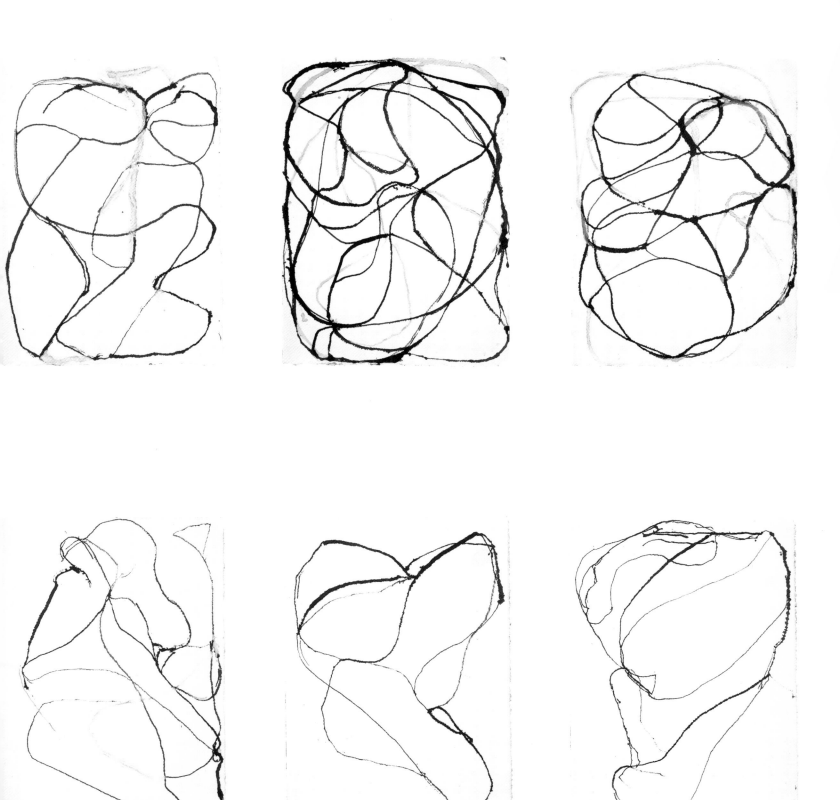

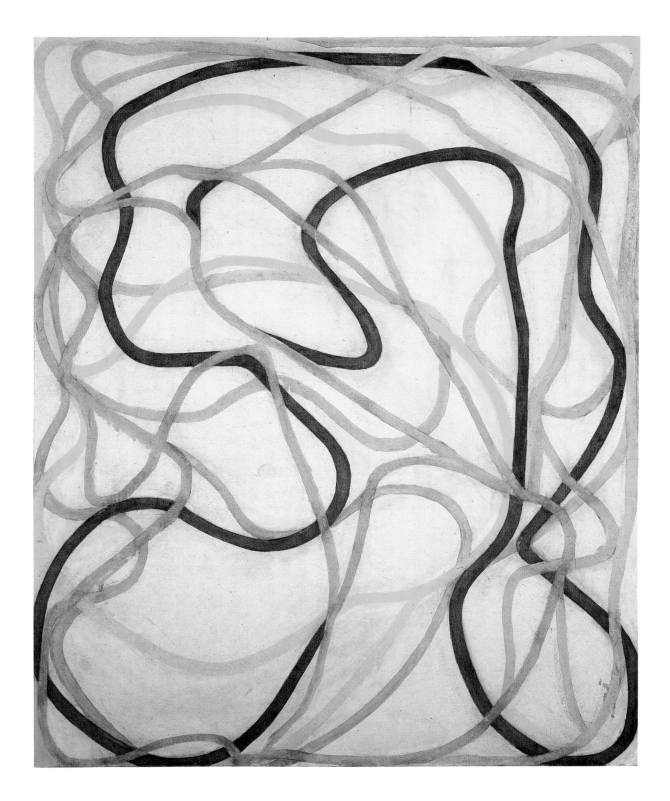

17.
Daoist Portrait
1993−95
Oil on linen
180.3 × 134.6 cm
Private collection

18.
Skull with Thought
1993–95
Oil on linen
180 × 144.8 cm
Keith and Katherine Sachs

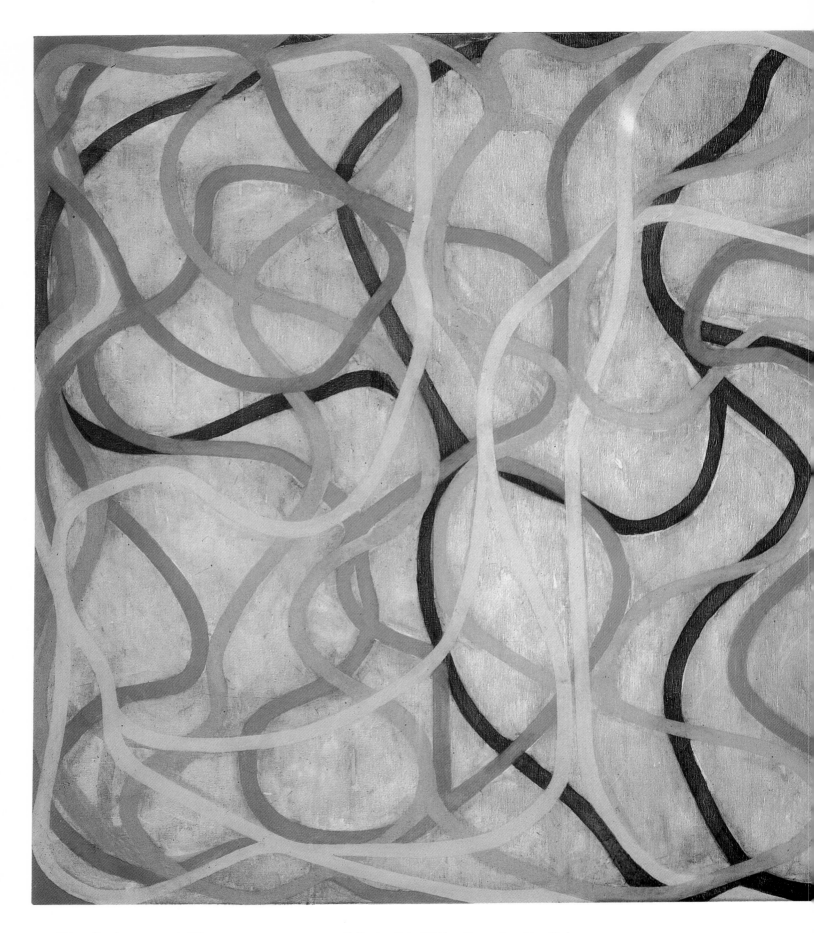

19. *Chinese Dancing* 1993–96 Oil on canvas 155 × 274.3 cm Collection PaineWebber Group, Inc., New York

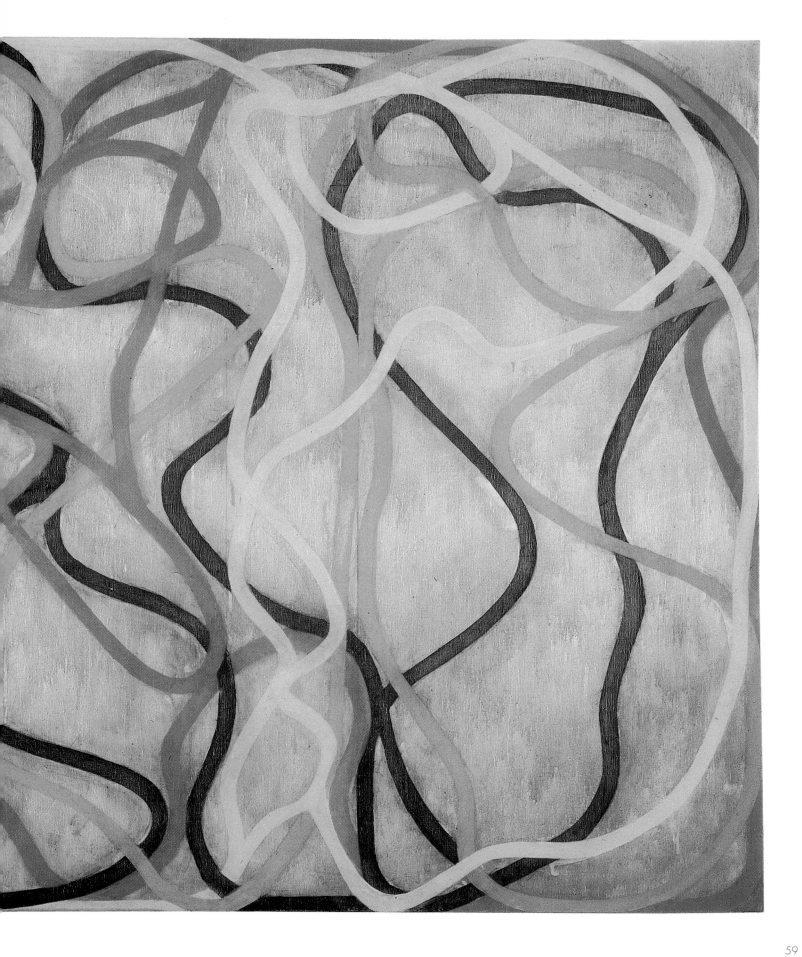

20.
Attendant
1996–99
Oil on linen
208.3 × 144.8 cm
Helen Marden

21.

Attendant 2

1996–99

Oil on linen

208 × 145 cm

Dr Paul and Dorie Sternberg

22.

Attendant 3

1996 – 99

Oil on linen

208 × 145 cm

Private collection, Switzerland; Courtesy Thomas Ammann Fine Art, Zurich

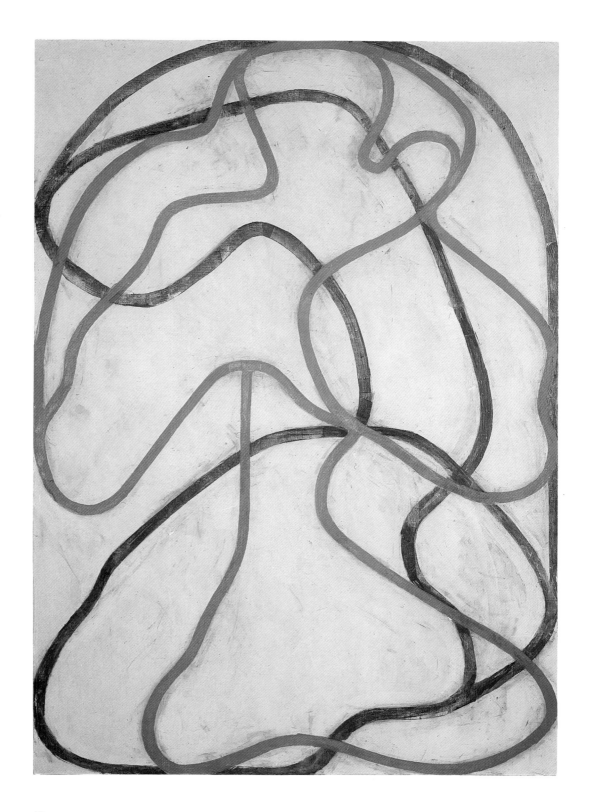

23.

Attendant 4 (Monk)

1996–99

Oil on linen

208 × 145 cm

Private collection, Courtesy Thomas Ammann Fine Art, Zurich

24.
Attendant 5
1996 – 99
Oil on linen
208 × 145 cm
Private collection, Baltimore MD

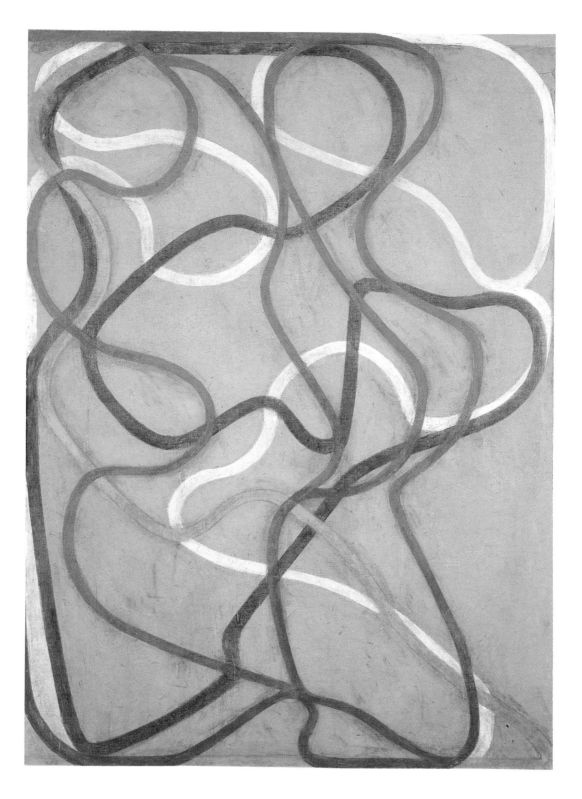

25.
The Attended
1996 – 99
Oil on linen
208 × 145 cm
Collection of the artist

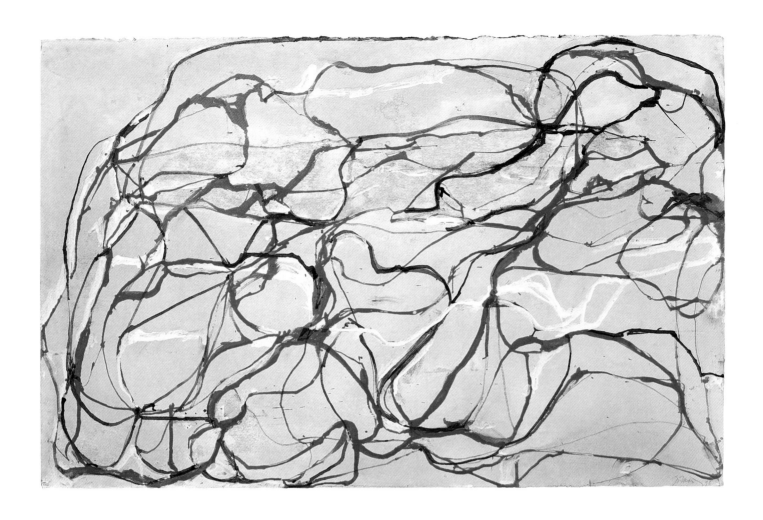

26.
Untitled Red and Green Drawing 2
1998
Hand applied wash ground and Kremer inks on Lanaquarelle paper
51.1 × 76.2 cm
Paul F. Walter

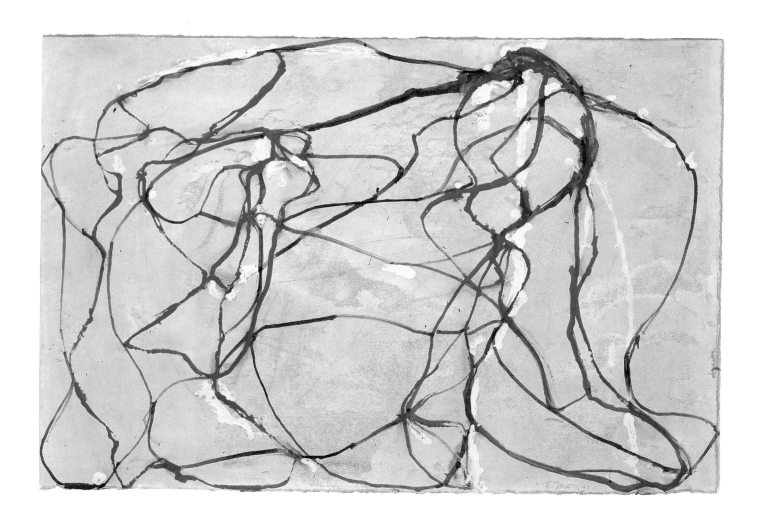

27.
Untitled Red and Green Drawing 3
1998
Hand applied wash ground and Kremer inks
on Lanaquarelle paper
51.1 × 76.2 cm
Collection of the artist

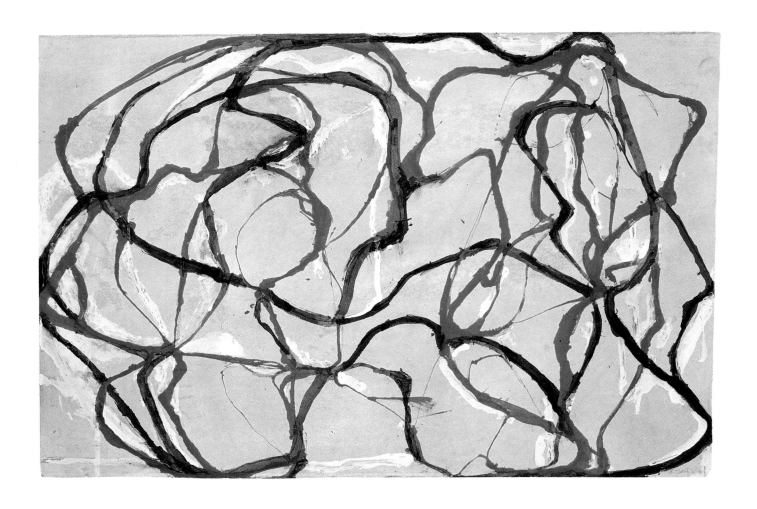

28.
Untitled Red and Green Drawing 4
1998
Hand applied wash ground and Kremer inks
on Lanaquarelle paper
51.2 × 75 cm
Private collection

Biography

Brice Marden was born in 1938 in Bronxville, New York and grew up in Briarcliff Manor. He attended Florida Southern College, Boston University School of Fine and Applied Arts (BA Fine Arts 1961), and Yale University (MA Fine Arts 1963). He lives and works in New York City and on the island of Hydra, Greece. Marden has continually engaged the tenets and practices of abstraction, first through his series of monochrome panels and drawings from the 1960s, 1970s and early 1980s, and subsequently through the line-based work he has been producing since 1985.

Selected one person-exhibitions of Brice Marden's work in public galleries and museums:

1974
Brice Marden Drawings, 1964–1974
Contemporary Arts Museum, Houston; Gallery of the Loretto-Hilton Center, Webster College, St. Louis; Bykert Gallery, New York; Fort Worth Art Museum; The Minneapolis Institute of Arts

1975
Brice Marden
Solomon R. Guggenheim Museum, New York

1981
Paintings, Drawings and Prints 1975–80
Stedelijk Museum, Amsterdam; Whitechapel Art Gallery, London

1991
Connections: Brice Marden
Museum of Fine Arts, Boston

Brice Marden – Cold Mountain
The Dia Center for the Arts, New York; Walker Art Center, Minneapolis; The Menil Collection, Houston; Museo Nacional Centro de Arte, Madrid; Kunstmuseum, Bonn

1992
Brice Marden: Prints 1961–91
Tate Gallery, London; Musée d'Art Moderne de la Ville de Paris and The Baltimore Museum of Art

1993
Brice Marden
Kunstmuseum Basel, Museum für Gegenwartskunst; Museum Friedericianum, Kassel

Brice Marden: Paintings 1985–1993
Kunsthalle, Bern; Secession, Vienna; Stedelijk Museum, Amsterdam

Brice Marden: A Painting, Drawings and Prints
The Saint Louis Art Museum

1997
Work Books 1964–1995
Staatliche Graphische Sammlung, Munich; Kunstmuseum Wintherthur, Switzerland; Wexner Center for the Arts, Columbus, Ohio; Fogg Art Museum, Cambridge, MA

1998
Brice Marden Drawings: The Whitney Museum of American Art Collection
Whitney Museum of American Art, New York

1999
Brice Marden: Work of the 90s
Dallas Museum of Art, Texas; the Hirshhorn Museum and Sculpture Garden, Smithsonian Institution, Washington, DC; the Miami Art Museum; the Carnegie Museum of Art, Pittsburgh, PA

Serpentine Gallery
Funders & Benefactors

The Serpentine is very grateful to
the following funders and benefactors
for their continued commitment.
This invaluable support enables
the Gallery to realise its ambitious
exhibition and education programmes.

Honorary Benefactors
Gavin Aldred
Brian Boylan
Ivor Braka
Noam and Geraldine Gottesman
Stig Larsen
George and Angie Loudon
Peter Simon

Benefactors
Simon Bakewell and Cheri Phillips
Tom Bendhem
Roger and Beverley Bevan
David and Janice Blackburn
Blains Fine Art
Anthony and Gisela Bloom
John and Jean Botts
Frances and John Bowes
Amber and James Bowles
Dan Brooke
Benjamin Brown
John and Susan Burns
Jonathan and Vanessa Cameron
Jonathon P Carroll
Christie's
Michèle Claudel-Maier
Dr and Mrs David Cohen
Loraine da Costa
Cathy Curan
Neil Duckworth
Mr and Mrs Mark Fenwick
Harry and Ruth Fitzgibbons
David and Jane Fletcher
Bruce and Janet Flohr
Forward Publishing
Eric and Louise Franck
James Freedman and Anna Kissin

Albert and Lyn Fuss
Barbara Gladstone
Glovers Solicitors
Francesco Grana and Simona Fantinelli
Sir Ronald Grierson
Richard and Odile Grogan
Richard and Linda Grosse
The Bryan Guinness Charitable Trust
Philip Gumuchdjian
Mr and Mrs Rupert Hambro
Mr and Mrs Antony Harbour
Mr and Mrs Rick Hayward
Thomas Healy and Fred Hochberg
Mr and Mrs Michael Hue-Williams
Montague Hurst Charitable Trust
Nicola Jacobs and Tony Schlesinger
Howard and Linda Karshan
King Sturge & Co
James and Clare Kirkman
Mr and Mrs Tim Kirkman
Mr and Mrs Charles Kirwan-Taylor
Mickey and Jeanne Klein
Rosemary Kowalski
The Landau Foundation
Barbara Lloyd and Judy Collins
Steve and Fran Magee
Karim Manji
Peter and Elena Marano
The Lord and Lady Marks
Catherine Martin
James and Viviane Mayor
Georgia Oetker
Omnicolour Presentations
Ophiucus SA
Mr and Mrs Nicholas Oppenheim
Linda Pace and Laurence Miller
Desmond Page and Asun Gelardin
Kathrine Palmer
William Palmer
Andrew Partridge
George and Carolyn Pincus
Ben Pincus
Mathew and Angela Prichard
John and Jill Ritblat
Dr and Mrs Mortimer Sackler
Alan and Joan Smith
Martin and Elise Smith
Sotheby's
Ian and Mercedes Stoutzker

The Thames Wharf Charity
Timothy Taylor Gallery Ltd
Mrs Britt Tidelius
Barry and Laura Townsley
UBS AG
Mr and Mrs Leslie Waddington
Robert and Felicity Waley-Cohen
Audrey Wallrock
Anthony Weldon
Lord and Lady John Wellesley
Robin Wight and Anastasia Alexander
Richard and Astrid Wolman

And Benefactors who wish to remain
anonymous

Founding Corporate Benefactor
Bloomberg

Corporate Benefactor
c-quential, an Arthur D. Little company

The Serpentine Gallery
Education Programme
is supported by

The Arthur Andersen Foundation,
The Diana, Princess of Wales Memorial
Fund and The Woo Charitable
Foundation.

With additional generous support from
John Lyon's Charity, The Paul Hamlyn
Foundation.

And kind assistance from The Baring
Foundation, The Calouste Gulbenkian
Foundation, The David Cohen Family
Charitable Trust and The Goldsmiths'
Company.

Serpentine Gallery Renovation (1996–1997)

The Serpentine Gallery renovation has been generously funded by The National Lottery through the Arts Council of England and The Baring Foundation, The Bridge House Estates Trust Fund, The Diana, Princess of Wales Memorial Fund, The John Ellerman Foundation, The Esmée Fairbairn Charitable Trust, The Henry Moore Foundation, The Department of Culture, Media and Sport, The Pilgrim Trust, The Foundation for Sport and the Arts and The Dr Mortimer and Theresa Sackler Foundation

Serpentine Gallery Board of Trustees

Lord Palumbo *Chairman*, Felicity Waley-Cohen & Barry Townsley *Co-Vice Chairmen*, Marcus Boyle *Treasurer*, Patricia Bickers, Michael Bloomberg, Roger Bramble, Marco Compagnoni, David Fletcher, Zaha Hadid, Isaac Julien, Joan Smith, Colin Tweedy

Serpentine Gallery Staff

Director's Office
Director
Julia Peyton-Jones
Assistant to the Director
Wendy Lothian

Administration
Head of Finance
Mark Failles
Finance Officer
Stephen Crampton-Hayward

Bookshop and Publications
Bookshop and Publications Manager
Ben Hillwood-Harris*
Assistant Bookshop Manager
Ruth Northey

Development and Press
Head of Development and Press
Kathy Stephenson
Development Officer
Louise McKinney
Press and Publicity Officer
Rose Dempsey
Events Co-ordinator
Natasha Roach
Press Assistant
Anna Barriball*

Education
Head of Education
Vivien Ashley
Education Co-ordinator
Andrew Fisher*
Temporary Education Co-ordinator
Julia Russell*

Exhibitions
Chief Curator
Lisa Corrin
Exhibition Organiser
Achim Borchardt-Hume
Exhibition Organiser
Leigh Markopoulos
Temporary Exhibition Assistant
Katherine Green*

Gallery and Building Management
Building Manager
Mark Robinson
Gallery Manager
Michael Gaughan
Weekend Duty Manager
Andy Shiel*

Gallery Assistants
Victoria Bicknell*
Jane Burke*
Jeanette Cleary*
Lawrence Corby*
Claire Cousins*
Kerry Duggan*
Mark Harris*
Nicola Holloway*
Caroline McCarthy*
Charlotte Newman*
Rory Snookes*
Vicky Steer*
Ib Vindbjerg*

(*Part-time Staff)

This catalogue is published to accompany the exhibition

Brice Marden

Serpentine Gallery, London
17 November 2000 – 7 January 2001

Curated by Lisa G. Corrin
Prepared and published by the Serpentine Gallery, London 2000
Edited by Lisa G. Corrin
Produced by Leigh Markopoulos

Designed by Herman Lelie
Typeset by Stefania Bonelli
Production co-ordinated by Uwe Kraus GmbH
Printed in Italy

ISBN 1 870814 47 9

Serpentine Gallery
Kensington Gardens
London W2 3XA
Telephone: +44 (0)20 7402 6072
Fax: +44 (0)20 7402 4103
www.serpentinegallery.org

Photographic & copyright credits

AKG Berlin / S. Domingié; AKG London / Erich Lessing; Prudence Cumming
Associates; Hans Humm, Zurich, 1995; Philippe Migeat © Centre Georges
Pompidou
All other photographs courtesy the lenders and Matthew Marks Gallery

The publishers are grateful for permission to illustrate the work of artists whose
copyright is represented as follows:
Jean Dubuffet © ADAGP, Paris and DACS, London 2000
Frantisek Kupka © ADAGP, Paris and DACS, London 2000
Piet Mondrian © 2000 Mondrian/Holtzman Trust c/o Beeldrecht, Amsterdam,
Holland & DACS London

The publishers have made every effort to contact all holders of copyright works.
Any copyright holders we have been unable to reach, or for whom inaccurate
acknowledgement has been made, are invited to contact the publishers.

The exhibition has received
significant support from
**Edwin C. Cohen and
The Blessing Way Foundation**

Sponsored by

Gap Inc.

In association with

The Daily Telegraph

With additional kind assistance from
the specialist art & antiques insurer

Nordstern
ART

Frances and John Bowes